TABLE OF CONTENTS

I	Start Smart	7
II	Selecting an Aquarium	11
III	Selecting Equipment for Your Tank	15
IV	Selecting Plants for Your Tank	25
V	Selecting Fishes	33
VI	Livebearers	37
VII	Schooling Fishes	43
VIII	Cichlids	53
IX	Scavengers	57
X	Anabantoids	61
XI	Goldfish	66
XII	Collecting Your Own Aquarium Fishes	69
XIII	Tank Maintenance and Feeding	75
XIV	The Educational Aquarium	81
XV	What if Your Fishes Get Sick?	87
XVI	When all is Said and Done	93

© 1982 by Dr. Herbert R. Axelrod   ISBN 0-87666-800-7

Hemichromis bimaculatus male guarding his eggs. Photo by Hans Joachim Richter, Leipzig, D.D.R.

ACKNOWLEDGMENT

The author is deeply indebted to Edward C. Taylor for the majority of the text. His editing job resulted in almost a complete rewrite of the original text, and had not the cover been pre-printed with my name alone, I would certainly have asked him to join me as co-author. However, the selection and captioning of the photographs from among the thousands in our files were done without his assistance.

PHOTOGRAPHY:

FRONT COVER: Jack Dempsey with fry, by Hans Joachim Richter. BACK COVER: Swordtails and cardinal tetras, by Hans Joachim Richter. FRONT ENDPAGES: Blue gourami, cultivated color variety, by Hans Joachim Richter. BACK ENDPAGES: *Nothobranchius* fire killie, by Hans Joachim Richter. All photographs of aquarium products are by Vince Serbin.

The aquarium products shown in this book are those which are internationally advertised in *Tropical Fish Hobbyist* Magazine. Their appearance in this book does not constitute the author's endorsement of these products. Your local aquarium or pet store expert is best suited to advise you on which equipment you should acquire for the location, size and configuration of your aquarium. These needs vary depending upon the variations of ambient room temperature, the pH and hardness of the water in which the fishes will be kept, and the amount of light available as well as the interaction of the fishes themselves.

Distributed in the U.S. by T.F.H. Publications, Inc., 211 West Sylvania Avenue, PO Box 427, Neptune, NJ 07753; in England by T.F.H. (Gt. Britain) Ltd., 13 Nutley Lane, Reigate, Surrey; in Canada to the pet trade by Rolf C. Hagen Ltd., 3225 Sartelon Street, Montreal 382, Quebec; in Canada to the book trade by H & L Pet Supplies, Inc., 27 Kingston Crescent, Kitchener, Ontario N28 2T6; in Southeast Asia by Y.W. Ong, 9 Lorong 36 Geylang, Singapore 14; in Australia and the South Pacific by Pet Imports Pty. Ltd., P.O. Box 149, Brookvale 2100, N.S.W. Australia; in South Africa by Valid Agencies, P.O. Box 51901, Randburg 2125 South Africa. Published by T.F.H. Publications, Inc., Ltd., the British Crown Colony of Hong Kong.

The T.F.H. Book of TROPICAL AQUARIUMS

DR. HERBERT R. AXELROD

Marbled hatchetfish are peaceful but are difficult for the beginner to keep. Feeding them is a problem. Spawning them in your aquarium is almost impossible, as is sexing them. Photo by Dr. Herbert R. Axelrod.

I
START SMART

So this is your first aquarium! Certainly you want everything to go smoothly with no hitches. So far, you are on the right track. Since you are reading this book, you bought it specifically to learn how to go about setting up your tank. If you are a cautious, inquisitive type, then you are consulting this book *prior to* the purchase of any equipment. Read this material from cover to cover and then make your decisions based on the knowledge you have gained. You will probably learn something from this book—and it will probably save you money in the long run. One more thing: if you have tried aquarium keeping before without success, this book should send you on your way to a proper start. Let's begin.

First, let's explore your motivation for wanting an aquarium. Perhaps you visited a friend recently and saw his tank. It may have been a beautifully decorated exhibit replete with lush green plants, graceful pieces of driftwood, and magnificent specimens of colorful and active fishes. You were envious and immediately wanted to rush out and buy a tank of your own. On the other hand, you might know someone who prefers a different sort of arrangement—nothing fancy, just plenty of fish with lots of interesting things going on to hold you glued to the tank. It's better than televison and a lot more interesting. It's even educational.

Don't be frightened by the word "*educational*," for it aptly describes the benefits which can be derived from a novice fish-keeping experience. If you are a teacher, keep education in mind throughout each step of the set-up procedure; emphasize the fun involved (the education will take care of itself). If your aquarium is to be a class project, perhaps each student or a small group can be given specific duties such as selecting the equipment, setting up the tank, or choosing the fishes. A coordinated effort will result in success at all stages and thereby produce the desired effect. (See the chapter "The Educational Aquarium.")

There is always the chance that you are reading this book because you have received an aquarium as a gift. This is a thoughtful way for your friends or relatives to teach you the value of caring for living things. In each of us, there is an inborn need to communicate with the world around us. Learning about fishes and their requirements will give you a good lesson in objectivity which will serve you well throughout life. One of the most rewarding pastimes for anyone retired from a full-time activity can be an aquarium. It offers something to do, something to watch, something to care for. Medical experiments to lower blood pressure and to induce a general feeling of calmness and a sense of well-being have proved the therapeutic value of caring for and watching fish swimming in an aquarium. There is not much left in this world that can lay claim to reducing stress—thank goodness for aquariums!

As you can see, the answer to the question, "Who can benefit from an aquarium?" is that anyone, at any age, can find their own individual reason for setting up their first aquarium. It will be just as easy for the youngster as for the adult if a few simple rules and precautions are followed. Step-by-step directions for the entire procedure follow. Be sure to read each section carefully or you might miss an important point to prevent possible disaster at a critical stage of the operation.

There are many different types of aquariums designed to accommodate those living organisms which are being maintained. By far the most popular—especially with beginners—is the *community* tank. This implies that a variety of fishes from many different, unrelated groups are maintained—but all live together in a relatively stable and harmonious environment. There are several types of community tanks. Years ago, when the aquarium hobby was young there was very little equipment available. The aquarist was forced to improvise. Everyone strived to create an environment within the tank which closely approximated conditions in nature. Artificial means of filtration and aeration were scorned. Such a tank was called a balanced aquarium. There was supposedly a perfect balance of plants, fishes, and even freshwater invertebrates. These would utilize, give off and absorb equal quantities of oxygen and carbon dioxide. The water would remain "sweet," or purified, due to the natural filtration action of the live plants. Aquarists could brag that they had not changed water for years.

In practice, the balanced aquarium was like utopia—often strived for but rarely, if ever, achieved. A "modified" balanced community tank, on the other hand, can be set up and successfully maintained by virtually anyone. Essential component parts of such an aquarium include fishes, plants, decorative items, and modern equipment.

Your aquarium shop can show you many beautiful aquariums with styles, sizes, and prices to fit every budget or match any decor. They can even make aquariums to fit the exact dimensions of a corner in your room. Consult your local aquarium dealer if you have a specific requirement.

Willem Tomey of Holland, a well known aquarist and photographer, took this photo of his own aquarium in which the fishes were added to enhance the beautiful plants rather than having the plants enhancing the beauty of the fishes.

Noah's Ark in Paris specializes in the manufacture and sale of custom-made aquariums. Their brochure, part of which we have reproduced below, shows various aquariums in the locations for which they were designed, as well as a view of the front of their shop in Paris.

II

SELECTING AN AQUARIUM

A magnificent aquarium designed and built by the Pacagnellas in Bologna, Italy. All of the apparatus to maintain the aquarium, such as the pump, heater, nets, fish foods, remedies, etc., are stored in the hollow stand. Photo courtesy of Werther Pacagnella.

What size aquarium should you purchase? It depends, of course, on how much space is available and how much money there is to spend. The best sizes for an initial community tank are 20 gallons to 30 gallons. There is a rule of thumb that holds that the smaller the tank, the more difficult it is to properly maintain. Although the most popular size aquarium is the ten gallon, it is really too small to function as a typical community tank. A thirty gallon aquarium is a good choice, but the cost factor must be considered. As a consumer, the size is up to you—you must be satisfied with your selection. While a 10 gallon aquarium is more difficult to maintain than a 20 gallon one, it is by no means very difficult.

If you have selected a 20 gallon tank, you will have the choice of a 20 gallon high or a 20 gallon long. The difference is obvious at first glance. The dimensions of a 20 gallon high are 24 inches long by 16 inches high by 12 inches wide. The dimensions of a 20 gallon long are 30 inches long by 12 inches high by 12 inches wide. So you have the choice of a high tank versus a long tank. Whichever one you choose will affect all the contents of the aquarium. If you find yourself in a dilemma you may take the easy way out by buying a 30 gallon tank. Its dimensions are 36 inches long by 16 inches high by 12 inches wide. With this tank you have both length and depth. By the way, the 20 gallon tank doesn't contain 20 gallons of water; it is just an approximation. A gallon of pure water weighs about 8¼ pounds. One cubic foot of water weighs 62.4 pounds. A 20 gallon long contains 2½ cubic feet, or 18.7 gallons, when completely filled.

Modern aquariums are made of glass with molded plastic trim to give a finished look and to protect the edges of the glass (and the hands of the aquarist). The plastic trim may be wood grain, black, brown, or tan. Alan Willinger invented an all-glass tank with a stainless steel trim. A few firms make plexiglass tanks, but they are not as readily available as glass.

Dr. D. Terver of the Nancy Aquarium, associated with the University of Nancy, France, supplied this photograph of one of his displays. The fishes and the plants complement each other in a symphony of colors and movement.

It is important that you carefully inspect the aquarium you decide to purchase. Check for cracks, pits, flaws, uneven seams, and inadequate or improper sealing. Most tanks come with a limited guarantee, so it is important to test your aquarium with water as soon as possible. You may use this waste water to clean the tank, but do not use soap or detergents, just water and a soft cloth or towel. If there is sealant residue on the glass, it can be removed with a razor blade. When testing for leaks be sure the aquarium is on a firm, level surface, preferably the very stand or location on which it will permanently rest.

Your aquarium shop will have very necessary equipment to enable you to maintain an aquarium of crystal-clear water. Consult with your dealer on the type of equipment as well as the method of using it properly.

It is important that you check your aquarium when you buy it and after you get it home. If it develops a crack or leak en route to your home you don't want to ruin your floor with a large puddle of water! Dow Corning makes an excellent aquarium sealant, as do other manufacturers.

If you had to guess, would you think these *Lamprologus elongatus* were peaceable fish? They're not. They are nasty and defend their territory fiercely. Photo by Doris Scheuermann.

III

SELECTING EQUIPMENT FOR YOUR TANK

You may have purchased a stand for your aquarium or you may have an article of furniture which will serve as a stand. Either way, the location of your tank is important. It should never be placed directly in a window since too much light will cause the water to turn green with algae in a short time. Likewise, an area where people are constantly moving back and forth is unwise since the activity may frighten the fish. Ideally, the base of the aquarium should be 30 inches from the floor, with a higher level being more practical than a lower one. Double-decker stands are fine as long as fish that do not frighten easily are placed in the bottom tank. A maximum of 2 hours of direct sunlight is beneficial. More than that will overheat the water. The remainder of the light should be supplied by the bulb in the hood covering the tank.

Needless to say, you will find it necessary to purchase a good deal of equipment to set up your tank. While many items might be considered a luxury, others are a necessity. Carefully study the checklist of equipment below and discuss it with your local pet shop operator:

(1) Tank and stand
(2) Decorations, including background
(3) Gravel
(4) Air pump and related items
(5) Filter (various types)
(6) Heater and thermometer
(7) Hood with light
(8) pH kit, breeding trap, siphon hose
(9) Food, remedies, and book on fish diseases

These items are essential and it would be difficult to maintain a *modified balanced aquarium* without them. Let's look at each item and learn what is best for your situation.

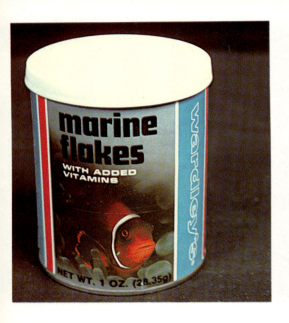

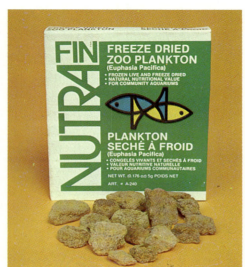
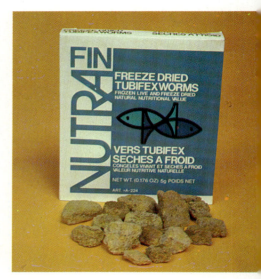

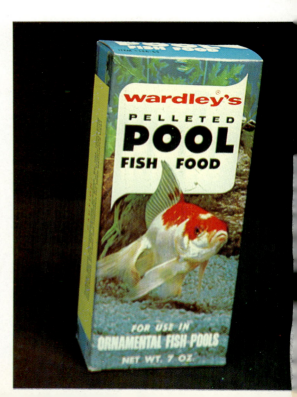

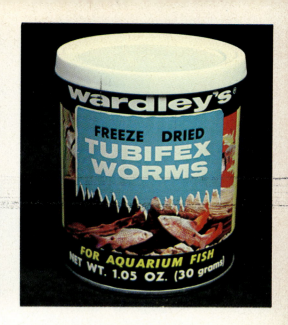

The fish foods shown on these pages represent only a small sampling of the foods and remedies available from a well stocked aquarium shop. There are literally dozens of fish foods, and you are well advised to vary your fishes' diet with different kinds of foods. The size of the particles of food you offer your fishes will vary with the size of the fishes and their eating habits. Discuss this problem with your pet shop specialist.

Various types of air valves are available at your pet shop. The ganged types are used for a more orderly arrangement. Many of them come with a plastic hanger to which the gang valves are fastened. The hanger fits over the aquarium's top frame.

Water purifiers and other chemical additives are available at your local aquarium store to assure good water for starting an aquarium.

Most undergravel filters and many other filters operate on the airlift principle, with air bubbles pushing water through a tube to lift it. The air bubbles are generated from a porous "stone" which is called an "air stone." These stones become clogged with dust after a relatively short period of time and must be changed or they will burn up the pump or stop releasing air. Depending upon the amount of dust around the air pump, your airstone should be changed monthly as part of your regular tank maintenance routine.

A siphon, especially a self-starting siphon, is an extremely handy gadget to have available for changing water or cleaning the tank bottom.

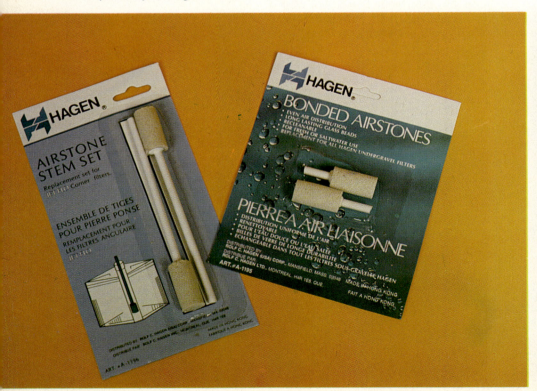

Platforms and shelves are available for storing your pump or other paraphernalia. Shown below is a typical colored gravel very popular with aquarists who want their tank to match the surroundings.

There are many beautiful aquarium backgrounds available. Select the one that best suits your needs.

We have already covered the tank selection adequately. Always place the tank near an electrical outlet. The back of the aquarium should be at least 10 to 12 inches from the wall so that there is room to reach behind it to adjust hanging equipment such as filters, pumps, or gang valves. Whatever the tank sits on must be sufficiently strong to support the weight of the entire setup. Since a 20-gallon long tank complete with sand will weigh about 175 pounds —enough said!

After you have tested your tank, select a suitable location and place the tank on its permanent base.

An essential part of any tank's decor is the **background**. While it may also be esthetically pleasing, it serves the useful purpose of providing security for the fishes. There is an endless variety of very colorful and interesting designs from which to choose. You may select a natural setting or simply a solid color motif. Backgrounds typically are taped to the outside of the tank; some are self-adhesive. You might consider a background of natural rock (usually shale) or some sort of molded design which hangs in the tank and thus plays an integral part in the tank environment. Many small cichlids (pronounced *sick-lids*) like to hide in the rocky crevices.

Next comes the **gravel**. There is a wide variety from which to choose. You may select for composition, texture, grain size, and color. Natural gravel is preferred by anyone wishing to create an atmosphere as close to the real thing as possible. This is an off-white, stone-colored gravel (usually #1 or #2 in grain size) which is simply crushed rock or natural riverbed stone. If you prefer a dark natural gravel you might try red flint. It will add a dash of color to the substrate. Mixtures of different gravels also look attractive. The amount of gravel you will require depends on the size of your aquarium and how deep you want the gravel. In general, one to two pounds per gallon is the correct range. Let's say you are going to employ an undergravel filter and/or maintain a large number of plants. Then you will want your gravel a bit deeper so the roots will have sufficient room to develop. In this case, two inches is necessary. If, on the other hand, you do not expect to use a large number of plants, you might make the gravel as shallow as one inch.

Before adding the gravel to the tank, it must be thoroughly washed in warm tap water to remove all the dirt and unwanted extraneous material. Several rinsings may be necessary before the waste water is clear. When this occurs, the gravel should be clean and ready to put in the tank. It is a good idea to buy a 2- or 3-gallon plastic bucket strictly for aquarium use. The bucket can be used to remove and replace water in the tank. Never rinse gravel in a bucket which has had detergent in it.

Pour the clean gravel into the clean tank and add enough water to just cover the top of the gravel. If you are using an undergravel filter you must place it in the tank *before adding the gravel*. Level the gravel so that it is of equal depth in all locations. You may now proceed to fill the tank about ¾ full. Be sure to use a **chlorine remover** or similar **water conditioner** to the water. Use water in the 80 to 85 degree (F.) range since you will be working in it for a while and there is no sense working in cold water. As you add the water, use your cupped hand or a soup dish to prevent the stream from scattering gravel all about. After you reach a certain water depth, the water itself will act as a cushion if you do not pour from too great a height.

It is now time to utilize a good deal of the equipment you have purchased. This will include: (1) the **air pump** itself, (2) **airline**, (3) a **gang valve**, and (4) a **pump hanger**. The air pump is used to introduce air into the aquarium. This may be accomplished through a filter or an airstone. The air is essential to the operation of a successful "*modified*" balanced aquarium. It creates a current which moves water from the bottom to the top and permits a greater exchange of gases at the air and water interface. In short, the dissolved oxygen content of the water is increased. Since fish extract oxygen from the water in order to breathe, it is important that the oxygen content be high.

You must select your **air pump** based on the number of air supply outlets you need. More powerful pumps cost more money. For the average 20- or 30-gallon community tank, three outlets are usually sufficient. Place your pump hanger on the back of the aquarium and set the pump on it. Run a piece of airline (plastic tubing) from the pump to the gang valve. Now connect each filter or airstone or other air-operated device to a piece of airline tubing and attach the pieces of airline tubing to the gang valve. Plug in the pump and adjust all outlets to a reasonable level. It is important that the pump be located no lower than the water's surface, for if it is lower there is a possibility that water could siphon into the pump if the power fails. Even if you intend to use a power filter instead of an inside filter, you can still employ an airstone to circulate the water better.

The next step is to put in the decorations and plants you have purchased. If you have decided on the natural approach, you will be using driftwood, rocks, and live plants. These should all be rinsed in tap water and the plants disinfected. Your pet shop will help you with the necessary disinfectant solution, usually potassium permanganate. If you are constructing caves with rocks be sure they are stable and will not collapse when any fishes start to dig the sand out from under them. Plants will be discussed in their own chapter.

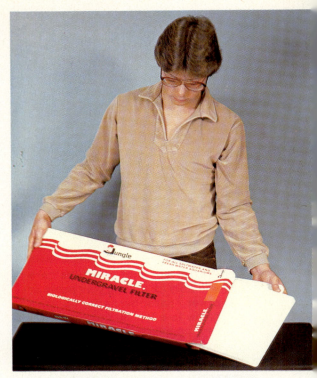

Undergravel filters are made to fit almost every standard-size aquarium. The undergravel filter should be purchased and installed when you purchase the aquarium, since putting in an undergravel filter after the tank is set up is almost impossible without completely uprooting the whole aquarium. If you decide to add filtration after your tank is set up, perhaps a water pump filter like the one shown below can be used. Setting up one of these filters does not require any disturbance of the original aquarium arrangement.

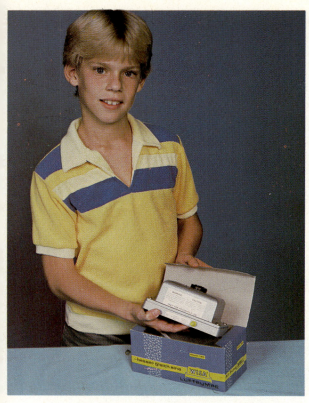

Air pumps are made in various sizes depending upon the output capacity you require. There are some very cheap pumps which are noisy and weak. Invest in a quality pump from the beginning and save yourself a lot of grief.

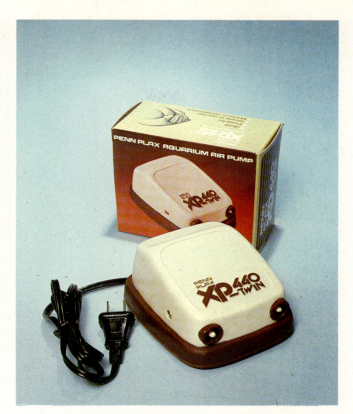

Some superior air pumps on the market have multiple outlets. The characteristics of a good vibrator air pump are how quiet they are, the ease with which the diaphragms can be replaced, the volume of air and pressure of air they produce, and whether the dealer will service the pump or whether you have to return it to the manufacturer.

A real "must" is an inexpensive water test kit which measures the acidity or alkalinity of the water. Neutral water has a pH of 7.0. Readings below 7.0 indicate that the water is acidic; readings above 7.0 indicate that it is alkaline. You will want to minimize the fluctuation of the pH of your aquarium.

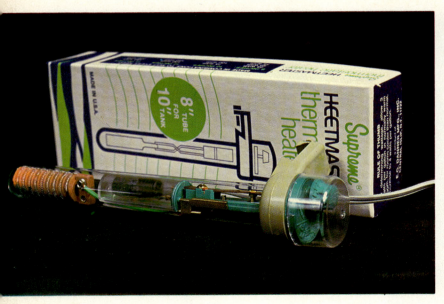

Thermostatic heaters are the best pieces of equipment you can use to maintain an even temperature in your aquarium during the colder seasons. A thermometer, as shown below, should be used in conjunction with the heater.

When your decision has been made to buy an undergravel filter, have your pet dealer show you how to set it up. Some filters are more difficult to set up than others.

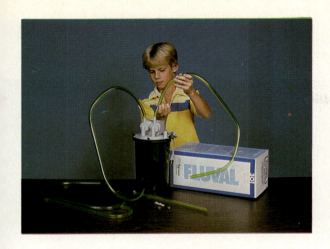

The three photos above illustrate three of the many power filters. These types of filters are more expensive than those filters driven by an air pump, but they are a great deal more efficient and powerful and they last for many years if properly serviced. Poor equipment has done more to harm the hobby of fishkeeping than any other single factor.

Take a final look at your completed decor and be sure you are satisfied with it. Add the rest of the water until the tank is full. It is quite likely that you have already placed a filter in the tank if you are using an **undergravel filter**. If you have decided on an inside filter or a power filter to hang on the back of the aquarium, now is the time to set it up. In a 20 or 30 gallon tank, two inside filters will be needed. A single power filter with two **airstones** in the tank will work equally well. Obvious constituents of any filter include **filter floss** and **charcoal**. Since you have already plugged in the **air pump** and the **power filter**, you will have probably recognized the need for an extension cord.

There are two popular types of **power filters** available today. One draws water from the tank through siphon tubes; the water flows through the filter material and is pumped back into the tank via an output tube. The other filters are called **overflow** models. They draw water in by a single tube and then push it through the filter material from the bottom up. It returns by cascading like a waterfall into the tank. Both work equally well, but the overflow type will work even when the water level in the tank is low. This provides a safeguard which many people prefer.

Everything, it is hoped, has gone well up until now. If so, you should place the **heater** in the aquarium and allow 60 minutes for it to reach the same temperature as the water. There are two basic types of heaters. One remains completely submerged while the other attaches to the side of the aquarium. Both work equally well, but the submerged type can be hidden better. Select the appropriate size heater by using the formula of five watts per gallon. Thus, a 20 gallon tank requires a 100-watt heater, and a 30 gallon requires 150 watts. Plug the heater in and turn the dial until the pilot light just comes on. Check the temperature with a thermometer which has been tested for accuracy. If the temperature is too low to suit you, simply turn the knob a notch or two (in the proper direction) and wait for the pilot light to go off. If the aquarium is warmer than the usual 75-78°F. you must wait for it to cool down before you set the thermostat.

Aside from the fish, the final touch is the **hood,** which should completely cover the tank. Across the back, a strip of flexible plastic is normally provided so cut-outs can be made to fit the equipment being used. A **lamp**, preferably fluorescent, will be situated in the middle, with a hinged flap in front to provide access to the tank. Your pet shop or aquarium store salesperson should show you how to set up all the accessories you buy.

Hans Joachim Richter's magnificent photograph of a male firemouth cichlid, *Cichlasoma meeki*, guarding his young. When planting rooted plants in an aquarium housing *C. meeki*, you must embed them within heavy pebbles so the fish cannot uproot them. Usually the male will uproot all the plants to clear his line of vision when guarding his fry.

IV
SELECTING PLANTS FOR YOUR TANK

Most novice aquarists want their first aquarium to look like a lush garden of aquatic vegetation. Little do they realize that keeping and growing plants successfully is a task equal to that of maintaining the fishes. In short, plants will thrive only if they receive the proper amount of attention. They cannot be expected to take care of themselves. The community aquarium should contain only those plant species which are hardy and adaptable to a variety of conditions. Perhaps the most important concession to a planted aquarium is the use of an undergravel filter. It will draw the necessary nutrients to the gravel, and thereby, to the plant roots. Adequate circulation of water is essential, as is a controlled quantity of both natural and artificial light. Most plants prefer water a bit cooler than do fishes, but this factor is perhaps the most flexible one.

When selecting plants, try to obtain those which will reproduce easily but will not outgrow the tank, or those which can be pruned effectively without killing the plant. You may consider four different categories of plants: (1) **bunch plants** - these are sold in bunches and may grow equally well both floating or rooted, (2) **single plants** -these are offered as individual specimens fully formed but not necessarily fully grown, (3) **bulbs** - these frequently have only a single short stem or none at all and must be planted under the gravel until they begin to sprout; many bulbs develop into large and beautiful plants in a matter of a few months, (4) **floating plants** - these may be bunch plants which are not rooted or any one of a number of small plants which can cover the surface like a blanket.

There are not many **bunch plants** which do well in the aquarium. Such plants as *Myriophyllum* (milfoil), *Elodea* (anacharis), *Eleocharis* (hairgrass), *Cabomba, Ceratophyllum* (foxtail), *Hygrophila,* and *Ludwigia* are almost always available and not expensive, but they are sunlight-grown and do not survive in the usual aquarium environment. Select no more than two species of bunch plants for your tank since uncontrolled growth may cut off light to other plants and leave little room for the fish. The versatility of

Left, upper photo: Tomey's photograph of one of his magnificently planted aquariums. Lower left: *Ceratophyllum demersum*. Lower right: *Cabomba caroliniana*. Both photos by Ruda Zukal.

Riccia fluitans, a floating plant. Photo by Zukal.

Lemna minor, a floating plant. Photo by Zukal.

Sagittaria subulata. Photo by Zukal.

Ceratopteris thalicroides. This plant is commonly called water sprite. Photo by D. Terver, Nancy Aquarium.

bunch plants makes them very popular. Using four to six stems per bunch, take a small piece of lead rope and press it gently around the stems about an inch from one end. Burrow this end into the gravel. You may also allow the plants to float, but this will mean a rather haphazard look.

Single plants are much less demanding than bunch plants, and by nature they are also a bit more spectacular. They may have leaves which are round, oval, or elongated -and red or green in color. Their variety is astounding and includes a number of species from many different groups. You might select such plants as *Vallisneria* (corkscrew val), *Echinodorus* (Amazon sword), *Sagittaria*, *Hygrophila*, *Ceratopteris* (water sprite), *Aponogeton*, and *Cryptocoryne* species. These must be planted in the substrate with the roots (but not the crown) completely covered. Don't crowd them! The broad-leaved plants require even more space. Short plants should be in the foreground and taller or more spacious specimens in the back. Groupings of the same species look very nice, especially the slender plants such as *Vallisneria* and *Sagittaria*.

Several types of **floating plants** are available if you wish to use them. In the community tank when a large number of rooted plants is being maintained, you will want to keep the floaters to a minimum. Otherwise, they might cut off too much light to the plants below. These unrooted plants tend to grow very fast, and they must be harvested frequently to prevent them from taking over the entire aquarium. Some of the plants you might consider are *Lemna* (duckweed), *Vesicularia* (Java moss), and *Riccia*.

Perhaps one of the best plants for the community tank is water sprite (*Ceratopteris*). It may be grown either rooted or floating. The physical appearance of the plant depends on where it is grown. Submerged plants have a very fibrous stalk with thin leaves. The floating plants have long, dangling roots with wide, soft leaves. This plant is considered an excellent indicator of water quality. If it flourishes, the water is probably healthy for the fishes; if it dies or does not grow, the water probably needs to be changed. At least one rooted specimen of water sprite is recommended for every modified balanced aquarium.

If you have decided to keep live plants in the aquarium, select fishes which will not eat those plants. There are numerous types of fishes which utilize plant matter as a major portion of their diet. Some of these will feed on flake food if it is offered and leave the plants alone. Others will be not so easily swayed and will eat not only the flake food but the plants as well. If you maintain tough-leafed plants primarily, any problems of plant-eating will be cut to a minimum. Unfortunately, many desirable plants are of the soft-leafed variety, so if you wish to keep these, you must select your fishes accordingly.

Submersed form of *Ludwigia palustris*. Zukal photo.

Vesicularia dubyana, an underwater moss attached to a piece of driftwood. Photo by Ruda Zukal.

Above, right: *Echinodorus horemani*. Zukal photo. Below, right: Water wisteria, *Hygrophila difformis*. Photo by Dr. D. Terver, Nancy Aquarium. Above: *Vallisneria americana*. Photo by T. J. Horeman. Below: *Myriophyllum spicatum*. Zukal photo.

Mr. Tomey set up and photographed this tetra aquarium in which the plants and fishes are in perfect balance and harmony. The skill of Mr. Tomey as an aquatic gardener is very evident from the many magnificent aquascapes he photographs. There is a greater art and skill in growing plants like these than in caring for the fishes.

Facing page: These three photographs were made by the author in Nancy, France at the famous University Aquarium. They show the different aquarium setups. The topmost photo shows a tetra tank, plus a few dwarf cichlids, all from Africa. The plants are short. The center photo shows fishes from southeast Asia, while the bottommost photo depicts a Brazilian cichlid tank showing a rocky aquarium and no plants.

The wide majority of fishes that occur in nature live in environments where there is a good deal of aquatic vegetation. Some of the exceptions to this rule would be the tetras from very acid waters where plants cannot grow, and cichlids from the rift lakes in which there are very few species of plants. It is by no means necessary to keep live plants in your aquarium, although if you want to maintain a modified balanced aquarium, plants are essential. If you choose **plastic plants**, you will find a wide variety from which to select. Many of these are extremely realistic copies of actual species; others can be found in brilliant colors which exist in no living aquatic plants. It is your choice to make. The fish will probably care very little as long as cover is provided by either plastic or live plants. Mixing live plants with plastic plants works well but is totally unacceptable to purists!

These young *Semaprochilodus taeniurus* are not meant for the small aquarium, nor for one which is not covered. The author collected these fish at night in Brazil when they jumped about 8 feet above the surface of the water into his boat, one of them hitting him in the face. Photo by the author.

V

SELECTING FISHES

The time has finally arrived to purchase fishes for your aquarium. Your tank should be set up for at least 48 hours before you begin to add fishes. Be sure the water is perfectly clear and all filters are working properly. The water temperature should be in the 75°-80° F. range. Check to see if the pH is between 6.8 and 7.2. If all factors are "go" - you may proceed. To some extent this is the easiest part of the entire tank set-up operation. It is certainly the most exciting. You might merely select the fish you like rather than opting for specific types. Such haphazard selections usually result in problems, but few community tanks are totally problem-free. You must be ready to accept the fact that not every fish you buy will prove to be a suitable resident. Some will be too aggressive, others too timid. On the whole, however, relatively few problems will occur if you follow the suggestions of a knowledgeable pet dealer.

There are over 8,500 species of freshwater fishes which constitute about 41% of all bony fishes. Many of these are found in tropical waters - so you see that for the tropical freshwater community aquarium, you have literally thousands of species to choose from. Not all of these will be available, of course, so you must be satisfied with what can be purchased in your local pet shops. That figure should run to hundreds of species and be more than enough to suit virtually everyone.

This is one of the great achievements in breeding livebearers—a sphenops molly with both a lyre-shaped tail and elongated ventral fins. The fish was bred in Singapore and photographed by Yeok Ong.

This highly cultivated male wagtail swordtail will probably develop cancer. The black pigment cells usually develop into a carcinoma. The author became interested in fishes while studying about the black cancer known as melanoma. The laboratory animals used for the cancer research were swordtails and platies, and it was during this research in the laboratories of Dr. Myron Gordon that most of the present-day platy and swordtail varieties were developed.

Certain types of fishes are better for the community tank than others. The distinction may be due to size, breeding habits, feeding requirements, or temperament. For instance, if a fish would outgrow its tankmates and maybe even its tank, it would not be a good choice. Some fishes become very territorial and aggressive when they breed, and these may destroy not only other fishes but the aquarium decor as well. Predatory fishes might eat their tankmates and are, therefore, not recommended. Other fishes are very timid and prefer to hide a great deal; these could easily starve to death in a community tank. An extremely interesting, colorful, and varied assortment of fishes can be selected from five groups of fishes. Each group has the distinction of being relatively easy to maintain; they accept a wide range of water conditions and eat almost anything. Also, these fishes are comparatively non-aggressive and relatively inexpensive. Let's look at them now.

Guppies are the "typical" tropical fish. Most people who do not have fishes have never heard of a platy or molly, but everyone has heard the word "guppy." The female guppy shown above is relatively colorless. She is shown here with her week-old baby. Male guppies, shown below, are extremely colorful; many color strains have been and are constantly being developed.

A beautiful group of swordtails and platies. All of them have been developed with fins that are much longer than normal. Long-finned varieties are much more difficult to breed than the normal variety because the anal fin of the male fish becomes distorted and is unable to function as an intromittent organ. Photo by Dr. K. Knaack.

VI

LIVEBEARERS

Livebearers are probably the most popular fishes for beginners. They give birth to free-swimming young which are miniature reproductions of the female when they are born. These fry are relatively large for newborn fish, and they are perfectly capable of taking care of themselves as long as their parents or other fishes in the tank do not eat them. When a female livebearer is noticeably heavy with young, she should be placed in a breeding trap where the young can be protected after they are born. There is no trick at all to breeding livebearers except that a male and female are necessary. These are easily distinguished since the male of the species has his anal fin modified into a breeding organ known as the gonopodium. The female's anal fin is typically wedge-shaped. One of the outstanding aspects of keeping livebearers is that you will find a huge array of different fishes available. There are actually only a handful of species involved, but they have been developed into a multitude of varieties by fish farms around the world. As it turns out, the genetic make-up of many livebearers is quite plastic and new strains can be created in only a few generations.

Most livebearers are capable of reproducing at between three and four months of age, so several generations can be produced each year. The most common livebearers include guppies, platies, swordtails, and mollies. *Poecilia reticulata* (guppy) is considered the king of all genetic-bred species for it is available in numerous colors with different fin shapes. Unfortunately, guppies do not make the very best community fish since the males are quite small and have very long, flowing fins which might be nipped by other fishes. This does not mean they cannot be kept, simply that a bit more care must be exercised in selecting their tankmates.

Perhaps better choices are the platies (*Xiphophorus maculatus* and *Xiphophorus variatus*) and swordtails (*Xiphophorus helleri*), which are closely related fishes every bit as desirable as the guppy. They reach 4-4½ inches in length and can take care of themselves. Mollies (*Poecilia latipinna, P. velifera, P. sphenops*) are very popular, but they prefer some salt added to their water and a diet high in vegetable matter. Also, they may grow quite large, and this could cause problems later on. Really, the choice is yours, and there is no good reason to reject any of these fishes, for their shortcomings are negligible.

A beautiful pair of blood-red swordtails. The male is the fish with the swordlike extension to his tail. The various strains of platies and swordtails freely interbreed. Photo by the author.

Top, facing page: A beautiful male sailfin molly. Below: A male swordtail displaying his fins in front of a female.

Above: A pair of lyretail mollies. On the facing page is a pair of blue wagtail platies. Blue is the only color in which mollies and swordtails have not been bred. The female is the larger of the two fish, and her anal fin is fan-shaped, while the male has a compressed pointed anal fin. Photo by the author.

Above: Head and tail light tetras, *Hemigrammus pulcher haraldi*. Below: The black neon, *Hyphessobrycon herbertaxelrodi*, named to honor the author. Photos by the author.

Hyphessobrycon erythrostigma, the bleeding heart tetra. Photo by Hans Joachim Richter.

VII

SCHOOLING FISHES

This is an artificial grouping which contains many different types of fishes, but all of them tend to swim in schools if their numbers are sufficient. Most of these fishes reproduce by scattering eggs, so they might alternatively be known as egglayers. It would be relatively unusual to spawn any of these species in the aquarium and have their fry survive, but the purpose of a balanced community tank is to observe the fish, not to have them reproduce. That can come later if you decide to specialize with a specific group of fishes.

When buying fishes which school, it is essential that you purchase six to eight individuals or they will not exhibit their schooling behavior. The major types of fishes which will be considered are tetras, barbs, rasboras, danios, and rainbows. Many of the species in these groups remain small enough at maximum size to be perfect for the community tank.

Tetras belong to the family Characidae, and they are found in South and Central America as well as Africa. They are on the whole small, colorful fishes which live in schools and are found in quiet, slow-moving waters. Except for a bit of fin-nipping, most small tetras can be kept without difficulty. You might wish to select from the following recommended list:

(1) *Hemigrammus caudovittatus*, Buenos Aires tetra
(2) *H. erythrozonus*, glowlight tetra
(3) *H. ocellifer*, head & tail light tetra
(4) *H. pulcher*, garnet tetra
(5) *H. rhodostomus*, rummy-nose tetra
(6) *Hyphessobrycon flammeus*, flame tetra
(7) *Hy. erythrostigma*, bleeding heart tetra
(8) *Hy. herbertaxelrodi*, black neon tetra
(9) *Hy. serpae*, serpae tetra
(10) *Cheirodon axelrodi*, cardinal tetra
(11) *Gymnocorymbus ternetzi*, black tetra
(12) *Paracheirodon innesi*, neon tetra

Barbs tend to be a bit more aggressive than tetras and grow a bit larger. They are mostly found in Asia and Africa, but the majority of the species in the hobby come from Asia. Color varieties and long-finned strains of barbs and danios have been developed. Some of the species available include:

43

A glowlight tetra, shown above. Photo by K. Paysan. To the right are tiger barbs, *Capoeta tetrazona*. Below are golden tetras, *Hemigrammus rodwayi* or *H. armstrongi*. The gold coloration is a disease in the skin cells of the fish which is not transmittable from fish to fish. When these golden fish are bred, the babies all develop into normal silver fish.

The fish above has been called many things over the years, since there are at least a dozen species that all look alike to the average aquarist. This particular species is *Hyphessobrycon callistus*. The fish shown below are Buenos Aires tetras, *Hemigrammus caudovittatus*. Photos by the author.

This piranha is not meant for the home aquarium, though it is very popular in Europe as a "pet."

Photo by Hans Joachim Richter.

(1) *Barbodes everetti*, clown barb
(2) *B. lateristriga*, T-barb
(3) *Capoeta semifasciolatus*, half-striped barb
(4) *C. oligolepis*, checker barb
(5) *C. titteya*, cherry barb
(6) *C. tetrazona*, tiger barb
(7) *Puntius conchonius*, rosy barb
(8) *P. filamentosus*, black-spot barb
(9) *P. lineatus*, striped barb
(10) *P. nigrofasciatus*, black ruby barb
(11) *P. ticto*, tic-tac-toe barb

A smaller number of barbs is necessary to form a school than with tetras, and since they are aggressive feeders, too many might eat more than their fair share. Of all the schooling fishes mentioned here, barbs are the worst fin-nippers. This does not mean they should be left out of the community tank; instead, they should be using sparingly, not in large numbers.

Rasboras and danios are cyprinids which are closely related. The major difference is that danios have barbels while rasboras do not. There is hardly a species of either which cannot be kept in the community tank. Schools of 6-10 fish are graceful and active, and mix well with all fishes. Danios swim almost at the surface while rasboras inhabit the upper to middle regions of the tank. Some of the species to look for include:

(1) *Brachydanio albolineatus*, pearl (gold) danio
(2) *B. rerio*, zebra (leopard) danio
(3) *Rasbora borapetensis*, red-tailed rasbora
(4) *R. cephalotaenia*, porthole rasbora
(5) *R. einthoveni*, brilliant rasbora
(6) *R. heteromorpha*, harlequin rasbora
(7) *R. kalochroma*, big-spot rasbora
(8) *R. trilineata*, scissortailed rasbora
(9) *Tanichthys albonubes*, White Cloud Mountain fish

Although a school of beautiful fishes can be a spectacular sight, it is probably unwise to mix too many species of schooling fishes together. Experimentation is the key to the right combination. The final group of schooling fishes which you may add to your tank are known as rainbows. They are in the families Melanotaeniidae and Atherinidae and their range is mainly restricted to New Guinea and Australia. They are different from other fishes in that they have two dorsal fins and remind one to some degree of minnows in the way they behave. Like *Rasbora*, rainbows can be said to be totally innocuous, and they will rarely harm, chase, or harass other fishes. A number of species are available and as the name implies, rainbows are extremely colorful fishes which deserve a spot in any community aquarium.

The serpae tetra, *Hyphessobrycon serpae*.

The flame tetra, *Hyphessobrycon flammeus*.

The rummy-nose tetra. There are at least three different species called by this name, and the scientific names are confused at the moment.

Facing page: Glow-line rasbora, *Rasbora pauciperforata*. Photo by Dr. D. Terver, Nancy Aquarium.

To the left is a long-finned white cloud mountain fish, *Tanichthys albonubes*. Below is the harlequin, *Rasbora heteromorpha*.

To the right is the zebra danio, *Brachydanio rerio*. Below is the black ruby barb, *Puntius nigrofasciatus*. All photos by Hans Joachim Richter.

The fish shown above is *Crenicara filamentosa*. This is a very poor photograph of a magnificent fish. The male shown above is not in good condition, nor are his fins expanded. The fish shown below is another Brazilian beauty, *Apistogramma agassizi*. These dwarf cichlids are very peaceful fishes. The fish to the right is the most popular of all dwarf cichlids, the ram, *Papiliochromis ramirezi*; the species is still known to many as *Apistogramma ramirezi*. The male is shown here herding his fry. Photos by Hans Joachim Richter.

VIII

CICHLIDS

The family Cichlidae contains over 1,000 species, and many of these are popular aquarium fishes. Unfortunately, a large number of them grow too large, are too aggressive, or dig up the gravel too much to be considered good community tank inhabitants. A group of neotropical species, however, grow no larger than four inches and rarely dig or attack their tankmates. These are commonly known as dwarf cichlids and include such species as:

(1) *Papiliochromis ramirezi*, ram (gold ram)
(2) *Apistogramma agassizi*, spade-tailed apisto
(3) *A. reitzigi*, Reitzig's apisto
(4) *Nannacara anomala*, golden dwarf cichlid
(5) *Crenicara filamentosa*, checkerboard cichlid

A few larger cichlids are peaceful and do well in the community situation. These include *Cichlasoma severum* (gold and regular), *C. festivum*, and the angelfish *Pterophyllum scalare*. Angels have been bred into a number of strains such as silver (wild), marble, blushing, half-black, black, zebra, and gold.

Many of the mouthbrooding cichlids from Africa, especially the riverine *Haplochromis*, may be kept if you are prepared for a good deal of digging activity. It is quite possible to breed mouthbrooders in a community tank and retrieve the fry. They frequently escape from their parents' mouths to prosper and grow up in the tank.

Finally, if you once again don't mind a bit of gravel rearrangement, the *Geophagus* species from South America are relatively peaceful even though they grow to a fairly large size. A community tank without cichlids is like a cake without icing. These highly evolved fishes exhibit interesting and diverse behavioral traits.

Cichlids tend to be territorial to a great extent, and this means they may try to defend a specific object in the tank, such as a rock or a piece of driftwood. If you have too many cichlids, it won't be long before they have the tank divided into a series of battle zones. Obviously, you must restrict the number of cichlids so that other fishes in the tank will be able to go about their business unhindered. It is best, therefore, to select no more than two specimens of any cichlid species.

Geophagus brasiliensis is a plant-uprooting cichlid. Richter photo.

Angelfish, undoubtedly the most popular of all cichlids, usually are peaceful.

IX

SCAVENGERS

The next group of fishes recommended for every community tank are the bottom-dwellers, also known as scavengers. These are primarily catfishes, spiny eels, loaches, algae-eaters, and some species of "sharks" (cyprinids in the genus *Labeo*). Catfish in the genus *Corydoras* are familiar aquarium residents and are totally peaceful. There are over 100 species of *Corydoras*, and many are available in your local pet shop. Other acceptable catfishes include the suckermouth species in the family Loricariidae, commonly known as plecostomus. Many catfishes grow too large for a community tank, so check with your dealer on which ones are suitable.

Loaches come in a variety of shapes and sizes, and small species such as *Botia sidthimunki, B. horae,* and all the kuhli loaches will add a touch of excitement to your tank. Likewise, most spiny eels are comical and harmless alternatives to the loaches. Be careful, however, for some eels grow too large for the community tank.

Corydoras paleatus, one of the armored catfishes, is an excellent scavenger. Photo by Hans Joachim Richter.

Botia macracanthus, the clown loach, is an excellent scavenger, perhaps the most colorful one, too. This peaceful fish comes from Indonesia. It grows very large, perhaps to 12 inches or more.

The red-tailed shark (*Labeo bicolor*) and the red-finned shark (*Labeo erythrurus*) make interesting additions to the community tank. They are constantly on the move searching every crevice for something to eat. Unfortunately, they tend to enjoy chasing other fishes through the tank. This sort of behavior gets out of hand sometimes, especially if there are two sharks. Limit your shark selection to a single fish.

INVERTEBRATES

Freshwater invertebrates usually are maintained as scavengers and are used for a value they supposedly have as cleaner-uppers of animal and vegetable matter that the aquarist doesn't want in the tank. The approach is a bad one, because the invertebrates are very interesting in themselves and often are worthy of as much study and care as the fishes—but it's the approach that currently has the greatest appeal among hobbyists.

Snails are the invertebrates most commonly found in freshwater aquariums. There are a number of different species that have attained some degree of popularity, and most of the popular snails do have a value as scavengers; that is, they can help to rid a tank of growths of algae, and they will consume animal matter (including dead fishes) that the fishes in the tank overlook. Some snails can get to be a problem, though, because of their tendency to reproduce too quickly and thereby give the tank too large a snail population; the pond snail *Physa* is an example of a potential troublemaker in this regard. Other snails present no danger at all of making a nuisance of themselves by becoming too numerous; the snails of the genus *Ampullaria*, for example, usually sold under the name "mystery" snails, are much harder to propagate than many fishes. Snails will eat fish eggs but pose no danger to healthy fishes except insofar as they serve as vectors for fish parasites, which they sometimes (infrequently under aquarium conditions) do. If you find snails interesting and would like to observe them in your tank, get some mystery snails. If you consider them to be pesty and potentially harmful, ask your dealer for a good snail eradicator and check carefully any live plants that you put into your tank; live plants often carry snails and snail eggs along with them.

The crustaceans popularly called crayfish or crawfish also are used as "scavengers" in freshwater tanks and are sold in many pet shops. Crayfish are very interesting animals and are the most efficient means available for ridding a tank of live tubificid worms that have become entrenched in the gravel; they also are great snail-killers. Unfortunately, crayfish have been known to kill fishes as well, and they are pure death on live plants.

One of the snails of the genus *Ampullaria*, generally sold under the name "mystery" snail. Photo by R. Zukal.

Crayfish make interesting scavengers. Photo by Dr. Herbert R. Axelrod.

The most popular of all air-breathers is the Siamese fighting fish, *Betta splendens*, which has been bred in just about as many colors as a rose.

The dwarf gourami, whether of the normal wild coloration or of the red strain recently developed, is known scientifically as *Colisa lalia*. Photo by Hans Joachim Richter.

X
ANABANTOIDS

These species are commonly known as bubble-nest builders or labyrinth fishes. They possess an accessory breathing organ which permits them to extract oxygen from the air. So important is this ability that fishes trapped below the surface will die, since their gills cannot extract enough oxygen from the water alone. There are three types of anabantoids to consider: (1) paradise fishes, (2) bettas, and (3) gouramis. Paradise fishes were one of the first types of tropical fishes kept in the home aquarium. They actually prefer relatively cool waters since they are found primarily in China, but they do well even at temperatures up to 84° F. There are only two species of paradise fishes readily available and one of these can be found in the albino form. *Macropodus opercularis* is the common paradise fish and *Pseudosphromenus cupanus cupanus* is the spike-tail paradise fish.

Only a single pair of these fish should be kept in a community tank. It is easy to distinguish the males from females since they are more colorful, and the fins have filaments.

Betta splendens, better known as the Siamese fighting fish, is one of the most popular aquarium fishes. Unfortunately, males tend to be very aggressive and cannot be kept together even in a large community tank. A male may be kept along with several females but you can expect the females to show some wear and tear from the male's chasing. One of the major drawbacks to *splendens* is the same one which applies to the paradise fishes: males of both species have long, flowing fins and can easily be nipped, ripped, or torn by various fishes in the tank. There are several other species of *Betta* in the hobby and any one of these would be a good choice for a community environment, although once again, only one male should be kept per tank.

Gouramis are extremely popular aquarium fishes and there are quite a few species available to the hobbyist. Virtually any of these are satisfactory for a community aquarium, but some grow considerably larger than others. Gouramis in the genus *Col*...

The giant gourami, also known as the thick-lipped gourami, is neither a giant nor does it have exceptionally thick lips when compared to the rest of the fishes of the genus *Colisa*. Photo by Hans Joachim.

reaching more than three inches in length, while gouramis in the genus *Trichogaster* may reach ten inches, but more normally grow to only six inches. Fish in either genus are acceptable although *Colisa* gouramis tend to be less aggressive, and more of them can be kept together. Some of the fishes you might wish to purchase include:

(1) *Colisa lalia*, dwarf gourami
(2) *C. chuna*, honey gourami
(3) *C. labiosa*, thick-lipped gourami
(4) *Trichogaster trichopterus*, blue (3-spot) gourami
(5) *T. leeri*, pearl gourami
(6) *T. microlepis*, moonlight gourami
(7) *T. pectoralis*, snakeskin gourami

The blue, or three-spot, gourami has been developed into several different varieties including the Cosby or marbled gourami, the gold, and the platinum gourami. Recently developed strains of the small species include the fire gourami and the golden honey gourami. If you decide to keep *Colisa* gouramis in your tank, you may keep more than a single pair of any species or you may keep several species together. With the *Trichogaster* types, it is advisable to have only a pair or trio of any one species per tank.

If you have decided to keep very small fishes in your community tank, there is another species of gourami which reaches only 1½ inches in length. This is the sparkling or pygmy gourami, *Trichopsis pumilus*. It does very well when housed with smaller, non-aggressive fishes. Do not try to keep it with any of the larger gouramis in the genera *Colisa* and *Trichogaster*.

Since gouramis are anabantoids, they will spend a certain portion of their time going to the surface and gulping air. When keeping labyrinth fishes in the community tank, you must be careful that the water's surface is not choked with plants. This might prevent the fish from obtaining sufficient air.

Favorite gouramis are: Left, *Trichogaster leeri*, the pearl gourami; top, center, the gold variety of the blue gourami, *Trichogaster trichopterus*; top, facing page, the dwarf gourami, *Colisa lalia*; center, facing page, the three-spot, or blue, gourami; bottom, facing page is the moonlight gourami, *Trichogaster microlepis*. Photos by H. J. Richter and the author.

XI

GOLDFISH

Many aquarists do not consider goldfish as an aquarium fish. This should not be. There are many exotic, bizarre and even grotesque forms of goldfish which must be maintained in the aquarium since they could not survive in the typical garden pool environment.

Besides adding color, goldfish are peaceful, hardy, relatively inexpensive and interesting. They, especially the small ones, are ideal for the community tank.

Ask your pet shop dealer to show you some of the various fancy goldfish varieties, some of which make great additions to the community aquarium. Feeding them is easy, too. They eat everything that you will normally offer your other community tank fishes whether it be live foods, frozen or freeze-dried foods or the more usual flake foods.

A goldfish that does equally well in a pond or an aquarium is the *azumanashiki*. This is a calico-colored goldfish with a lion's cap on its head and face, a double tail and beautiful coloring. The two insets show similar color varieties of the same fish strain. Photos compliments of *Midori Shobo*, Japan Fish Magazine.

The famous German photographer and author Hans Joachim Richter. He is shown in a real photograph, not posed or faked, as he actually stands in piranha-infested waters in order to catch them. Photo by the author.

The author, Dr. Herbert R. Axelrod, has discovered almost 450 new aquarium species and has traveled into 38 previously unknown rivers in Brazil to search for new fishes. Here he is travelling up an unnamed river in Brazil looking for something new. Photo by Willi Schwartz.

The author transferring fishes from the plastic boxes in which the fishes are placed as soon as they are caught, into a holding pen made of fish nets. Photo by Dr. Martin Brittan.

XII

COLLECTING YOUR OWN AQUARIUM FISHES

The *Ebenezer* has been the author's Amazon boat for almost 20 years. Shown here at Lake Tefe, the home of the green discus, the author takes a refreshing bath. The boat is slow, going about 10 miles per hour, but the crew operates 24 hours a day; it took about five days from Manaus to Tefe. This trip brought back 8,000 discus, 50,000 *Corydoras* and some assorted other fishes! Photo by Dr. Martin Brittan.

One of the greatest joys available to aquarists is the joy of creating life by breeding their favorite aquarium fishes. Nothing can compare with the feeling of pride and accomplishment that one receives from being responsible for adding more fishes to your collection from among those you bred.

Second to the joy of breeding fishes is the joy of collecting your own. Those lucky enough to live in the tropics can probably venture into the nearest ditch, pond or stream and in a few hours have some very beautiful specimens for their home aquarium. Usually they will have collected juvenile specimens of fishes which grow rather large, but occasionally they find some colorful fishes which are already in full color and in their mature size. Certainly Australian hobbyists are familiar with many of their indigenous rainbowfishes. Not only are these beautiful fishes to be found in most rivers and creeks in the northeastern section of the country, but random species are also found in New Guinea, and how beautiful they are!

American hobbyists have it much easier than their Australian counterparts. While a dozen or two Australian fishes make suitable aquarium inhabitants, the American darters, scores of them, are almost all suitable for the fish tank . . . and the tank doesn't even have to be heated! The easiest way to catch darters is with a small bait trap available at most bait stores or fishing shops. It usually pays to become friendly with your local fishing store owner and to find out what fishes he sells as bait. Quite often these fish are great aquarium inhabitants, especially the males when they are in full breeding colors, usually in the spring. Darters are not the only colorful American fishes suitable for the aquarium. Within 100 yards of the T.F.H. office in Neptune, N.J. is to be found one of the most colorful

The green discus which the author collected in Tefe, Brazil, with one of the local Indian maidens. She eats the discus as part of her natural diet. Photo by the author.

This large specimen of *Melanotaenia trifasciata* exhibits the typical non-courtship pattern with a faint mid-lateral band.

This small falls is on a tributary of the Jardine River on the Cape York Peninsula. It is the habitat of *M. trifasciata*.

Male and female specimens of *Melantaenia goldiei* from the Sogeri Plateau, Papua New Guinea.

Even females of *M. goldiei* are beautiful when kept in the aquarium.

Melanotaenia herbertaxelrodi is the only yellow species of rainbow, as this male attests.

The female *M. herbertaxelrodi*. This specimen was collected near Lake Tebera. New Guinea.

Photos by Dr. Gerald R. Allen, from *Rainbowfishes of the World*.

killies, *Fundulus heteroclitus*. This fish is sold as a bait fish with magnificent males and large egg-laden females sold as bait for fluke and weakfish fishing, and they are even used to capture crabs in special crabbing pots. A dozen beautiful specimens, alive and in good condition, can be purchased for the price of a packet of cigarettes. As more and more aquarists succumb to the pleasure of long distance air travel, it is not uncommon to find them searching the wilds of Brazil or Lake Malawi trying to catch their own really rare and exotic species. Under all circumstances, even when fishing in your own area, it is best to contact the local authorities (start with the local police) to ascertain whether permission is required to collect fishes in the waters you have selected. You might also contact the customs authorities in foreign countries to get permission to take live specimens out of the country, too. Your own native land might have restrictions about bringing in anything alive, so check that also.

Perhaps the greatest place in the world for collecting aquarium fishes is Brazil. Almost any place you go in Brazil will produce exotic, rare and beautiful aquarium specimens, but no place is better than the tropical parts of Brazil, especially those parts which are touched by the Amazon River. If you are fortunate enough to make it to Brazil, perhaps you might fly into Manaus on the upper Amazon. It has a jet airport and is a mere 4 to 5 hour flight from Miami, with direct connections to Europe, Tokyo and many cities in South America, especially Caracas, Venezuela, which has a daily flight. The hotels are good, the food is excellent (if you like fish) and the authorities usually are extremely cooperative if you want to collect only a few dozen small fishes.

Merely hire a taxi or small boat and ask to be taken to the nearest ditch (*igarape* it's called in Brazil). You'll always find a bunch of kids wherever you go in Brazil, so negotiate with them for a few token payments and ask them to fish for colorful fishes. Take along a good book which has plenty of colorful photographs of the kinds of fishes you are looking for, go through the book with your fishermen, and ascertain just which fishes are to be found in the area. It will probably amaze you how much these children know about the fishes in the area.

Once having collected the fishes, you should keep as few as possible in the largest plastic bag you can get. Your local pet shop will usually cooperate with you and show you how to hold and maintain the fishes in your hotel room with a plastic bag lining a Styrofoam box. The bag is sealed with a strong elastic band and this modest aquarium becomes its own shipping container. How proud you'll be to show your local pet shop owner the fishes you collected yourself!

The local kids always helped the author with his fishing. This tribe of Brazilian Indians, the Suya, are lip-disk Indians.

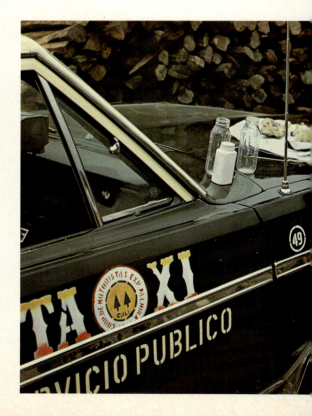

In Calima, Colombia, the author hired a taxi, collected fishes along the roadway, photographed them as he is doing here, then preserved them in formalin in babies' milk bottles. Photo by Heiko Bleher.

The author with famous Brazilian exporter Willi Schwartz who passed away in 1981. As fishes were collected in the jungle, the nets were used to fashion holding traps in which the fishes were stored until the boat came back to carry them to Manaus. Photo by Adolfo Schwartz.

Sometimes we didn't have ponds in which to store our fishes, so we fashioned temporary aquariums, using the shipping boxes as frames for the plastic bag liners. The fishes were kept in these boxes until the airplane came to carry them to Manaus. This setup enabled the boxes to be pre-packed, and it would only take a few hours to have 500 boxes of fishes ready for boarding the plane. Photo by Sue-rhea Pasca.

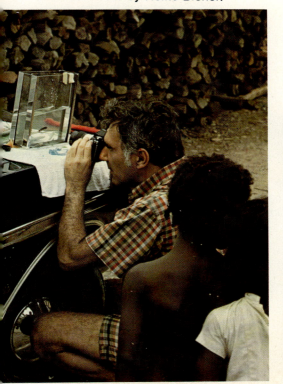

Top: A male *E. rufescens*, commonly known as the red snubnose darter. Bottom: The lowland snubnose darter, *E. pyrrhogaster*.

Top: A female *E. rufescens* from Pickens Creek in Missouri. Bottom: A female *E. pyrrhogaster* from Terrapin Creek in Tennessee.

Photos by Lawrence Page from the *Handbook of Darters*.

Top: A beautiful male *Etheostoma* that is presently undescribed. Bottom: The golden snubnose darter, *E. flavigaster*.

Top: A female of the undescribed species to the left. Even she has some color. Bottom: A female *E. flavigaster* from Little Sexton Creek in Kentucky.

XIII

TANK MAINTENANCE AND FEEDING

Well, now that your aquarium is full of fishes, or at least you are beginning to fill it up with fishes, it is time to consider the number of fishes you should keep in your tank. An old rule of thumb goes - *two inches of fish (tail excluded) per gallon of water*, but this rule can be broken with today's modern filtration and aeration. If a tank looks overcrowded, you can be sure that it is. If a tank looks sparsely populated, then it is probably understocked. What is recommended is that you try to purchase a variety of fishes which fill the different levels of the tank; the top, the middle, and the substrate, or bottom. For the bottom level, scavengers and barbs are the best choices. Many schooling fishes will swim in the middle to upper strata. In the upper level alone, you can count on danios and rasboras. Livebearers will tend to school in the center, if they school at all, since this phenomenon is not always manifest. You may find your livebearers located virtually anywhere in the aquarium.

A tank of southeast Asian fishes featuring gouramis, barbs and sharks. Photo taken at the Nancy, France aquarium by the author.

This magnificent window can be used to add decor to almost any type of surrounding. The circle is cut from wood and painted black. This gives shape to the magnificent setting of tall plants and cardinal tetras, *Cheirodon axelrodi*, one of dozens of fishes named to honor the author. Photo by Dr. D. Terver, Nancy, France.

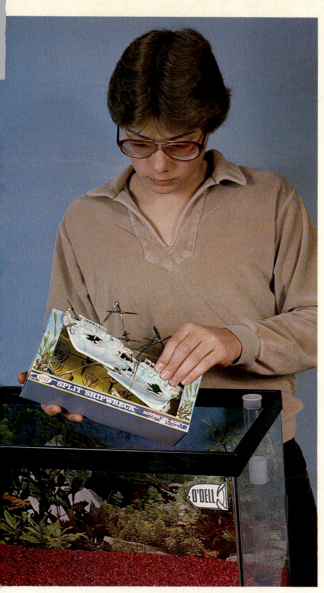

Your local aquarium store will have many ornaments, such as this sunken ship, to decorate the bottom of your aquarium. These bottom ornaments also function as hideaways for the more timid fishes.

If you have purchased too many fishes, you can be sure that problems will develop. The fishes will either reduce their numbers through aggression, or environmental conditions will deteriorate to the point that your fishes become diseased. If you wish to maintain even a moderately populated aquarium in perfect health, there are certain minimum maintenance requirements necessary. Tank maintenance is extremely important, and you cannot expect to neglect your fishes and have them remain healthy. Feeding your fishes on a regular basis is not enough. The single most valuable technique in maintaining a modified balanced aquarium is frequent partial water changes. If possible, 10-15% changes of water twice a week are recommended. If time does not permit this, a 25% change once a week is almost as effective. When removing old water from the aquarium always use a siphon hose and the bucket you bought strictly for aquarium use. If there is any debris lying on top of the gravel, siphon it off along with the old water. When you add new water to the aquarium, be sure it is at the same temperature or slightly warmer than the tank water itself. Always use a water conditioner to remove chlorine from the water. Add the water slowly to be sure it does not uproot any plants or disturb the gravel.

Any type of filter (except undergravel) which you have in the aquarium must also be cleaned on a regular basis. Depending upon the fish load, it will need to be cleaned once or twice a week. Remove the old charcoal and floss and throw it away, and replace it with new material (rinse the charcoal before use). If you are making frequent partial water changes, the water quality in your aquarium should not deteriorate. To be on the safe side, make semi-weekly pH readings just before changing the water. Should you find that the water has become too acid, it is important to make a larger water change to bring the pH back within an acceptable range. For the average community tank, this range is 6.8 to 7.2.

Another bit of tank maintenance is strictly esthetic in nature, but if algae start to grow on the glass or decorations, too much light may be reaching the tank. Remove the algae from the glass but leave them on the rocks for the fishes to pick on. Water which is starting to turn green has an algal bloom in it, and this may not be healthy for the fishes. There are chemicals you can add to the tank to kill this bloom, but a large water change will usually do just as good a job, and you will not have to worry about the residual effect of the chemicals.

The single most important factor which will unbalance your modified balanced aquarium is overfeeding. Most people love to feed their fishes, and it is not unreasonable to feed them four to six times a day. Fishes can live quite happily on two feedings a day, however, so if that is the number you have selected, feed them in the morning and evening. If you can feed them more often, feed them every four hours while the lights are on. Of course, it is recommended that the lights be kept on your aquarium between 12 and 16 hours a day. Should you leave the lights on constantly, you will get a bloom of algae, and the water will turn green. Also, constant light will not allow the fishes a resting or "sleep" period, and species which are not normally aggressive may become so. Yes, there are "cranky" fishes!

It is important that you feed your fishes no more than they can consume in 5 minutes. If there is any food left after 15 minutes, it should be siphoned from the aquarium. A wide variety of foods may be fed to fishes in a community tank. You have, it is hoped, selected these fishes partially based on their willingness to eat virtually any food offered to them. This would include semi-cooked or prepared foods in many forms, such as flakes, pellets, wafers, tablets, blocks, paste, etc. Also, frozen, freeze-dried, and live foods should be fed. Most of the common aquarium fishes mentioned in this book will accept all types of foods.

As you watch your fishes eating, you will notice that certain individuals or species do not seem to be getting their fair share. This situation can be rectified by modifying the food offered. As an example, if the fishes that are missing out are scavengers, and nothing is reaching the bottom of the aquarium, you might put in pellets or some other kind of heavy food which will sink directly to the bottom. If the fishes that are underfed are top-dwellers, you should put in food that floats longer. In this way, they will have first choice. If you notice that some fishes are not feeding at all, you have probably selected a species that is difficult to feed. Do not be dismayed. Undoubtedly, you will find some food, probably alive, that the fishes will eat. Then, the task is to see that they get their fair share. If they are picky eaters to begin with, chances are that the food they prefer will also be relished by every other member of the aquarium—and seeing that they receive enough to eat will be difficult. This, however, is merely one of the challenges and interesting aspects of maintaining fishes in the community situation.

Let us say you are feeding your fishes three times a day. The most varied diet possible is the best. In the morning you might feed frozen brine shrimp; in the afternoon, a flake food with a variety of different ingredients; and finally, at night, you could feed live food of some sort. Most live foods will continue to live in the aquarium if they are not eaten, and they will be available constantly. Although live foods cost a bit more than other foods, it is important that

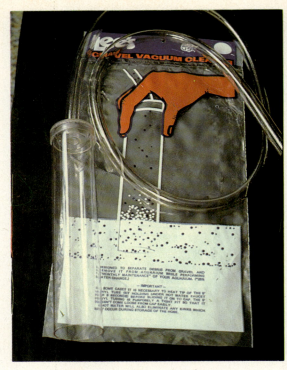

There are many plastic accessories which make aquarium maintenance easier. Your pet shop should have vacuum cleaners (above) and live tubifex worm feeders (shown below), plus many other accessories.

This aquarium is built into a wall and is used as a beautiful night light as well as a living decoration. One of the advantages of having recessed aquarium edges on tanks used in school situations is that it keeps the sharp edges away from children's fingers. Photo by Dr. Denis Terver, Nancy Aquarium.

Filters of any kind are only as efficient as the actual chemical and mechanical filtration materials they contain. Activated carbon or charcoal (above) is used to remove harmful gases and to remove the color which stains water from fishes' urine and from the dyes in fishfoods. Various filter wools, sponges, etc., are merely mechanical filters that remove particles suspended in the water.

your fishes receive at least an occasional treat of live foods, say, once or twice a week. Some of the live foods available include adult brine shrimp, brine shrimp nauplii (which you can hatch yourself at home), tubifex worms, white worms, earthworms, and *Daphnia* (which you may have to culture yourself). At certain times of the year, glass larvae will be available. A secondary hobby of collecting and maintaining cultures of live foods can be undertaken. Many aquarists enjoy this aspect of their hobby and find it an excellent way to supplement their fishes' diet, as well as learn a good deal more about how to maintain both the fishes and their foods.

You will find that the maintenance of your aquarium will become relatively easy if you set up a schedule for tank maintenance. Say—every Wednesday and Sunday night you elect to spend 30 minutes changing water, cleaning the glass, changing filter material, and checking the general condition of the fishes. This period of time can also be spent strictly in observation of the fishes and their behavior. It is hoped you will enjoy your aquarium to the extent that you spend a considerable amount of time watching the activity within. Fishes exhibit a wide range of behavior, and you can never be sure from one moment to the next what you will see. Unlike television, there is no guide you can consult to determine what the next activity will be—you must wait and see for yourself. The mystery and intrigue of nature is one of the major attractions of the community aquarium.

XIV
THE EDUCATIONAL AQUARIUM

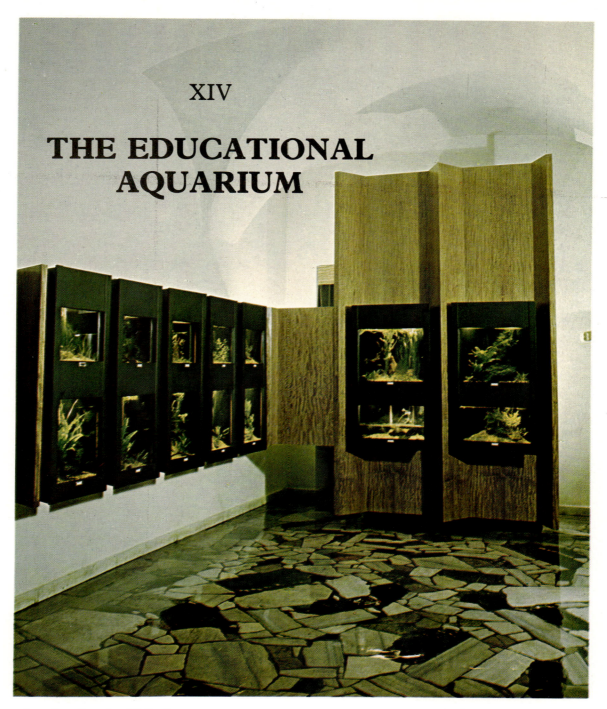

An educational exhibit of tropical fish can be extremely rewarding for schools, since it functions as a decoration for an otherwise blank wall, provides learning experiences for the students, and can be a producer of live materials for classes (algae, snails, tadpoles, fishes, etc.). Photo by Ruda Zukal.

In the spacious halls of a recently dedicated school there stands as a representative showpiece of a particular sort a huge aquarium with all the fine touches which modern techniques have made possible: the edges are hidden by an elegant wooden frame, the water temperature is exactly controlled by a thermostat and an invisible filter keeps the water crystal-clear. The plants gleam a lovely green in a perfectly balanced lighting. Among them scurry swift neon tetras, glowing like jewels. Majestic angelfish as well as other fascinating creatures hover there to charm the beholder. The installation was not cheap; its upkeep, aside from the electric current consumed, comes to a considerable sum of money in the course of a year.

The teacher or group planning to start educational aquaria must first give some thought to the purposes they should serve. That they are to serve as tools for instruction need not interfere with their esthetic value. An aquarium which produces a large amount of biological study material need not be unattractive. It should reflect as much attention as possible. Sloppy or neglected aquaria are certainly not the examples we want for orderliness among the students, nor do they cast a favorable reflection on the teacher! Better no aquarium at all!

Another question comes up: should the educational aquarium contain only native specimens, or should the popular exotic species also be kept there? Many of our youths (and their elders) have become dissociated from nature and, because of this, the native fauna should doubtless be given preference. Therefore, gather for the aquarium the frequently unnoticed or overlooked creatures from the ponds and brooks of the nearby countryside. However, do not exclude the exotic species altogether. They have interesting biological features, and students should not be deprived of their esthetic beauties.

In most schools fresh water aquaria are found almost exclusively, in spite of the fact that, especially in inland towns, a marine aquarium has a particular value. A new world unfolds, one with sea anemones, starfish, crabs and all sorts of other creatures of the sea. The care of a marine aquarium, of course, involves greater responsibilities. But today such a project is certainly within the realm of possibility for a school.

Where should the aquarium be located?

Show aquaria, when they serve a function besides decorating a home and when used to serve in educating students, can be situated in a lobby or hallway. Of course, it is usually necessary to resort to artificial lighting, so an electrical outlet, preferably a multiple one (for heating, lighting, aeration, etc.) must be handy. The location chosen must be such that the tank is not subjected to extremes of either heat or cold. Naturally, it must be out of the way of traffic, where no one can damage or overturn it by running into it. On the other hand, a group should be able to observe the aquarium without being disturbed and without hindering the passage of others.

The ideal solution, especially for a school, is to devote hall space to that purpose. By breaking through the wall between a hall and a room, the front glass will be exposed to view in the hallway. It is best to reserve the room for use as an aquarium room from which the servicing is done. The aquarium does not rob any space from the hallway, and the pleasant light given off from the aquarium is useful if the

This beautiful aquarium exhibit features well planted aquariums as well as labels which identify the contents of the aquarium.

passage is otherwise dark. Many public aquaria have long used this method of displaying.

The way the educational aquarium comes into its own is as a tool for instruction. In some elementary schools it is easiest to use an aquarium in a classroom, especially where every class has its own room and almost all instruction is given by one teacher. If the windowsills are not wide enough to hold an aquarium, use stands or sturdy tables. Schools which have a special biology classroom can be laid out to contain aquaria and terraria. A more difficult situation is encountered where a school has specialized teachers but no biology classroom. The biology teacher is then forced to set up aquaria in different rooms where he instructs perhaps only once or twice a week. This not only makes it more difficult to control the students, but sometimes teachers using the room for other classes are apt to complain that their students are distracted by the aquarium. There is no one solution—but perhaps setting up two aquaria in one or two rooms and shifting the students into these rooms for their biology classes is an answer.

With school aquaria, it is advisable to use signs to notify viewers what should be particularly observed, especially if only one class participates actively and the others are only casual observers. The signs can be made by the students from sturdy cardboard—sometimes with simple sketches. In making the signs:

1. Use scientific as well as popular names of fishes and plants.
2. Mention the place of the species in the scientific system.
3. Letter special remarks such as whether useful or harmful, kinds of nourishment, ecology, description of larval form, etc . . .

The students should be active participants when an aquarium is set up and maintained. Collecting the plants and whatever goes into the aquarium from local ponds and brooks will acquaint students with the conditions under which things are found. Decisions can be made beforehand as to how the native aquarium is to be set up so that its inhabitants can be accommodated.

Whether to entrust the outfitting of the aquarium to the entire class or to only a few especially interested or apt students is a decision best made by the teacher—and this depends on the nature of the class. In any case, the teacher will have to enlist the dependable assistance of a few students to maintain the aquarium, because he cannot do (and does not want to do) everything himself. The careful performance of the never-ending tasks, such as keeping the aquarium clean (cleaning the glass and siphoning the bottom), providing food, feeding, etc., when done by the students, is a potent aid in assuming responsibility and

Hexagonal impact-resistant acrylic plastic aquariums are ideal for schools, since they can be manufactured to any size or shape and are much less likely to break or hurt a student than an all-glass tank. Photo courtesy of Truvu.

growing up. Any carelessness shows up in short order: animals and plants die, algae run wild and the water begins to smell badly.

The maintenance of aquaria by students is a great means for promoting care, punctuality, and a feeling of responsibility. The teacher might perhaps appoint a large (or preferably a small) group and name them as caretakers of the aquaria. Then any carelessness can be assessed against this group, but if the aquaria flourish it goes to their credit. Control by the teacher should be as unobtrusive as possible, but care must be taken that the students do not spend too much time at the task and neglect their other duties and studies. Care must also be taken that the students do not endanger themselves when collecting food or aquarium specimens; the teacher must consider very carefully what he is asking the students to do without supervision. He should be well acquainted with the insurance provisions before he organizes any "pond excursions" or organizes any tasks to be done in the school.

How is a school aquarium maintained during vacation? The native inhabitants can be released before the vacation period starts, but what about the exotics, which must have constantly controlled heat? Sometimes one can find a janitor to take care of the aquaria. Perhaps it might be possible to find the fishes a temporary home outside of the schoolroom. In the larger cities sometimes members of aquarium societies are available. (In any case, it is a good thing to be on good terms with an aquarium society.) As these groups are interested in new members, they are usually ready to help. Society members are often useful in providing animal and plant life and are a valuable source of information and advice. It would be best if the biology teacher himself were a member of an aquarium society.

In any case the teacher must be certain that the elementary rules of animal care are not violated. The aquarium inhabitants must never be neglected, even temporarily. The love of wildlife which a child may have should be developed and encouraged by the care of an aquarium, rather than killed by neglect.

A child should also have his understanding and sympathy awakened for small creatures. If it becomes necessary to put a sick fish to death, it should not be done in the presence of the students, at least the young ones. Sometimes children become attached to living things they have had for a long time; the teacher can tell them afterward that he put the fish out of its misery quickly in order to spare it unnecessary suffering. When releasing native aquarium inhabitants for the summer, they should not be placed in merely convenient places, but should be brought back to the same natural haunts from which they were taken.

A tank containing aggressive cichlids, with the back wall of the tank and the rocks covered with algae. The algae grow just from the presence of an abundant light source. Photo by the author at Nancy, France.

A neon tetra showing white spots on its fins; these white spots are characteristic of "ich," the most common aquarium fish disease.

XV

WHAT IF YOUR FISHES GET SICK?

It is inevitable that no matter how good a job you do of maintaining your aquarium, at some point you will have a problem with sick or diseased fishes. This is not to be looked upon as a failure, but merely the fact that most living things deteriorate as they grow older, and older organisms tend to have more problems. If you are maintaining your water quality by frequent partial water changes and monitoring your pH, you should be able to circumvent problems for a considerable length of time. One of the ways that diseases can be brought into the aquarium is on the live plants which you are using. These should be thoroughly disinfected with a strong solution of potassium permanganate before they are placed in the aquarium.

The introduction of new fishes is probably the single most common way in which problems are brought to an already established tank. Frequently, a fish will be sick, but there will be no outward manifestations of the problem. It will only gradually become apparent over a period of several days or weeks.

Basically, there are two types of problems which you will have to deal with when it comes to fish diseases. These are parasitic infestations and bacterial or fungal infections. Many fish parasites are visible on the body of the fish after they reach a certain stage of development or have multiplied to a sufficient extent. Once you have detected these visible spots, it is up to you to determine what they are and treat accordingly. The most common aquarium parasite is *Ichthyophthirius multifiliis*, better known as ich. It manifests itself by forming numerous white spots on the body and fins of the fish. It is easily cured using several different drugs. Ask your pet shop dealer which drugs are best for your particular situation. Another disease similar to ich is velvet—caused by the parasite *Oodinium*. This disease is a bit more difficult to cure, but it can be done if you are diligent. The best drug to use is acriflavine. Again, ask your pet shop dealer what he uses.

You will find that several of the drugs used to combat parasitic infestations, such as acriflavine, contain a dye, and they will discolor your water. When you are using drugs with dye bases, it is important that you discontinue the use of charcoal filtration so that the dye is not absorbed by the charcoal and thereby rendered ineffective. It will still be important to maintain filtration, however, so you simply remove the charcoal from your filter and put the floss back in. You may need to add gravel or marbles to an inside filter to hold it down. Once you notice that the spots have disappeared for five days or more, you may consider the treatment completed, and it is then a good idea to change as much as 75% of the water.

Bacterial infections often become complicated by fungus. Basically, when the tank environment deteriorates to the extent that a bloom of bacteria has occurred, the bacteria attack weak fish or an open wound and kill selected areas of flesh. Fungus soon grows on this dead flesh. If you notice small, white tufts of hair-like filamentous material on your fishes, they have a fungal infection. There are many drugs available at your pet shop which will cure fungal infections. Be careful when using some drugs (including dyes); the packages will carry information as to whether they are safe for all types of fishes. In some cases, certain drugs may kill your plants. It is always recommended that if only one or two fishes in a community aquarium are infected, these should be removed immediately to a small treatment or hospital tank, so the drug will not have to be used in the main tank. This will save money since you will be using less medication, and it will go a long way to ensure that other fishes are not exposed to the same disease.

One of the things you might have to consider when determining what has caused a particular problem in your aquarium is the age of the fishes. Most livebearers live only two to three years, so if you have purchased, mature fish initially, it is likely that it may be reaching the end of the line. This can be determined by several signs of old age such as weight loss, subdued colors, hump-backs, and abnormal swimming motions. At this point, it might be best to remove the fish before it dies in the tank and causes additional problems in the community aquarium.

You will always experience a problem with fishes chasing one another, being aggressive, and, on occasion, doing bodily harm. This usually results in a few missing scales or torn fin membranes, but sometimes a fish may be damaged severely, and unless treatment is instituted, the fish may die. It is important, therefore, that you scan your aquarium a few minutes every day to ascertain if any particular problems are arising between tank inhabitants. If you notice a fish which is particularly aggressive and is harassing one or

A paradise fish which has both an external and internal bacterial infection which is beyond curing. The puffiness of the fish's body indicates an internal infection. Photo by Zukal.

This zebra danio is consumptive, as evidenced by its shrunken-away body. Nothing can save fishes like this. This is the way old fishes fade away. Photo by Zukal.

A wagtail hi-fin swordtail starting to develop the black cancer which almost always attacks this strain. Photo by the author.

The pox-like eruption on the head of this *Datnioides* was very contagious. Fishes with any external symptoms of disease should be isolated in an isolation aquarium (even a large glass jar will do, as will a plastic bag). Photo by the author.

The side of this *Bedotia geayi* has been infected from a small wound which became serious. *Bedotia* and other fishes from brackish waters often have problems when kept in community tanks. Photo by Zukal.

A barb showing a heavy infestation of *Oodinium*. When fishes are as infested as this one, it shows a very advanced state of the disease that should have been noticed and treated much earlier. Photo by the author.

This catfish has a terrible infection and should be destroyed. Photo by the author.

This golden tetra has a disease which shows up as discolored patches on its body. The disease actually is the golden color which is produced by skin parasites in the skin cells; the white blotches are actually healthy skin. The gold disease is, however, not debilitating, and this fish should not be considered ill.

This *Brochis* catfish is ill. Its fins are droopy, there are some small bloody patches on the bases of the fins; also, the slime coating of the fish is peeling off. This is probably a bacterial infection, and the fish should be removed and destroyed. Photo by the author.

This beautiful *Hemigrammus* has a wound on the head. The wound was then infected with bacteria which killed some of the tissue; *Saprolegnia* fungus subsequently attacked the dead tissue. This condition is easily cured if properly treated. Untreated fishes will die. Photo by Zukal.

more fishes, you may decide to get rid of it by trading it back to your dealer or a friend, or even giving it away. Trying to remedy the situation in any other manner may prove unsatisfactory. If the marauding fish happens to be one-of-a-kind, you might buy it a partner, either male or female, and see if it will take out its aggression on that fish. Usually, this aggression will not be as severe as that perpetrated on other species. Tank dividers are available to compartmentalize your aquarium. Your pet shop or aquarium store has these, too.

Your selection of fishes will be critical to the success of your aquarium, but you should not expect to make all the right decisions at first. After some time, you will learn which fishes you like and which you don't like, and you will become familiar with the disposition of each species. It is inevitable that you will want to purchase more of the fishes you like and get rid of those you do not like.

There are many excellent books on fish diseases. It is important that you get a copy as a reference guide so you can identify the problem and its solution as soon as possible. First aid for your fishes can save many times the value of a fish disease book.

Look closely and you might find fish lice attached to your fishes. The louse shown here on the body of a stickleback is difficult to see, since it is basically a transparent organism.

Fungus attacks dead *Corydoras* eggs. Unless the dead eggs are removed the fungus might grow over the live eggs, too. Photo by Hans Joachim Richter.

This African *Synodontis* catfish has a very strange disease which isn't too obvious when the fish is viewed from the side, but when the fish is viewed from above (see right) then the growths and loss of fins become very obvious. This is an unknown disease. It affected several hundred catfishes. Photo by the author.

XVI

WHEN ALL IS SAID AND DONE

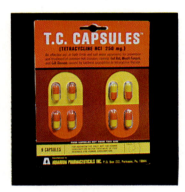

Your pet shop will have excellent remedies (usually antibiotics) to offer you for the treatment of most fish diseases, but you will need a book to know which diseases you must treat.

This is the philosophical section of the book. It is here that we can summarize the marvelous and wonderful things that tropical fish keeping can do for you. As with everything else in this world, it is not a panacea (cure-all). Not everyone will become infatuated with these lovely little creatures that cruise back and forth in their watery kingdom. If you give them a fair chance, however, the odds are that you will become a lifelong aquarist. As the title of our first chapter intoned—"*start smart.*" If you have read this book from cover to cover, and the idea of setting up an aquarium appeals to you, go and do it. Even if you already have that aquarium, this book should be of some help.

Let's face facts. There are only three ways to learn about something: (1) learn by doing it yourself, (2) learn by asking someone how to do it, or (3) learn by reading about it. There are few people willing to sit down and take the time to explain in detail how you should set up your aquarium. Even your local pet shop dealer would be hard pressed to have enough time to answer every question posed to him. Striking out on your own and learning by hit and miss or experimentation can be a very expensive proposition. This statement is not intended to discourage you from trying new things. Try them in moderation and listen to the advice of those who have been over the same ground, but why invent the wheel all over again?

In a short time, it will become apparent that this book is a good source for refreshing your memory. It will not take long for you to assimilate the concepts and learn about the fish and soon you will be on the way to becoming a successful aquarist. If you "*start smart*" be sure to "*stay smart*" by continuing to read as much as possible. TFH publishes a large number of books dealing with all aspects of the aquarium hobby, and if you have a specific area of interest, they have the books for you. And don't forget *Tropical Fish Hobbyist* Magazine, published monthly, to keep you up-to-date on what is happening in the hobby. It offers hundreds of informative and entertaining articles every year which are illustrated with the best photos in the world.

Good luck with your tank and fish! Enjoy!! **T.F.H.**, by the way, stands for **Tropical Fish Hobbyist**.